3836

BEGINNING LEVEL

Forty-one selections from around the world, chosen for their beauty and ease of performance. Certain to delight the beginning student.

(1st-3rd year ability)

WORLD FAVORITES

Printed in Canada

MMO CD 3836

Music Minus One

WORLD FAVORITES
Music Minus One Trumpet, Beginning Level

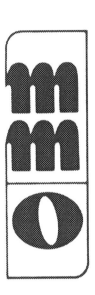

IN THE GOOD OLD SUMMER TIME

4 bar piano intro
precedes solo.

GEORGE EVANS

Tempo di Valse

3836

MY WILD IRISH ROSE

4 bar piano intro
precedes solo

CHAUNCEY OLCOTT

Tempo di Valse

SWEET MOLLY MALONE

8 bar piano intro
precedes solo.

Allegretto

IRISH SONG

TO A WILD ROSE

4 bar piano intro
precedes solo

EDWARD A. MACDOWELL

3836

THE YELLOW ROSE OF TEXAS

Brightly

COWBOY SONG

BECAUSE

GUY D'HARDELOT

PANIS ANGELICUS

CESAR FRANCK

4 bar piano intro
precedes solo

Poco lento

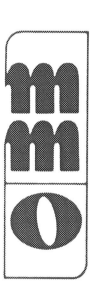

GLOW WORM

2 bar piano intro
precedes solo.

PAUL LINCKE

ETUDE

3 l4 bar piano intro
precedes solo.

FREDERIC CHOPIN, Op. 10, No. 3

Poco lento

LONDONDERRY AIR

2 1l2 bar piano intro
precedes solo

IRISH MELODY

Moderato

3836

Black Is The Color Of My True Love's Hair

2 bar piano intro
precedes solo.

FOLK SONG

GREENSLEEVES

1 2/3 bar piano intro
precedes solo.

ENGLISH FOLK SONG

3836

DEEP RIVER

2 bar piano intro
precedes solo.

Rather slow

SPIRITUAL

RED RIVER VALLEY

3/4 bar piano intro
precedes solo.

Slowly

TRADITIONAL

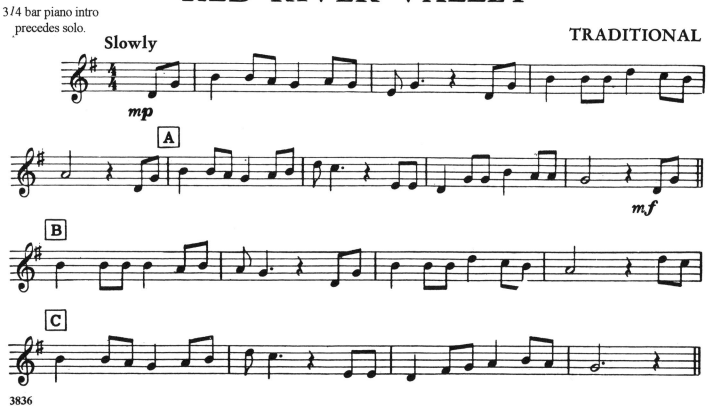

3836

MIGHTY LAK' A ROSE

2 bar piano intro
precedes solo.

Slowly, with expression

ETHELBERT NEVIN

3836

TO A WATER LILY

4 bar piano intro
precedes solo.

EDWARD A. MACDOWELL

3836

CHICKEN REEL

JOSEPH M. DALY

THE BIRTHDAY OF A KING

2 bar piano intro precedes solo.

Moderato

W. H. NEIDLINGER

NEARER, MY GOD, TO THEE

SIDE A - BAND 7

LOWELL MASON

2 bar piano intro precedes solo. **Moderato**

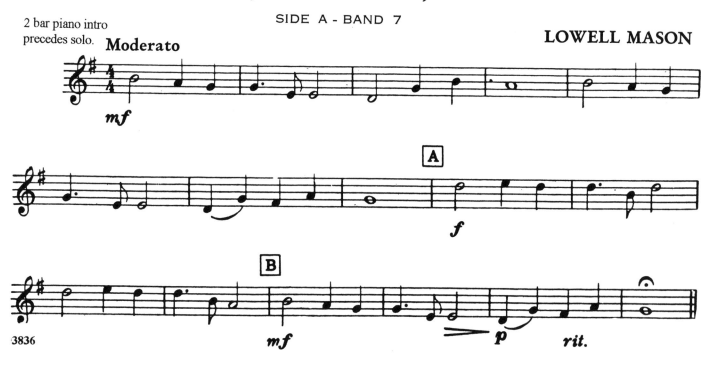

3836

He's Got The Whole World In His Hands

Moderato

TRADITIONAL

3836

PARADE OF THE TIN SOLDIERS

SIDE B - BAND 1

LEON JESSEL

2 bar piano intro
precedes solo

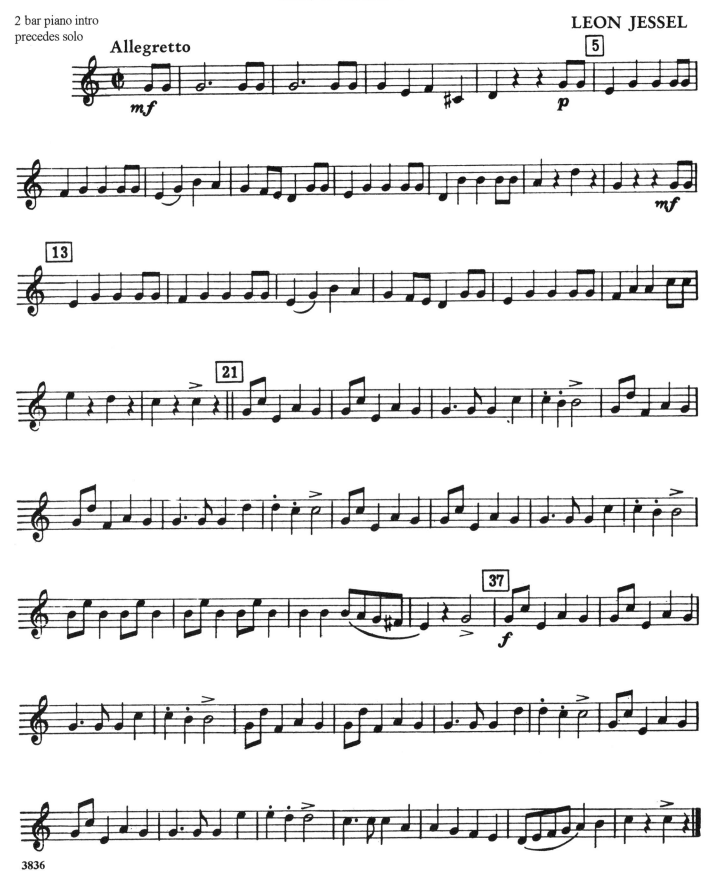

3836

THE MARINES' HYMN

U. S. MARINE CORPS SONG

3836

CAISSON SONG

U. S. ARMY SONG

March tempo

ON THE BANKS OF THE WABASH

PAUL DRESSER

FLOW GENTLY, SWEET AFTON

J. E. SPILMAN

3836

CLAIR DE LUNE

1 bar piano intro
precedes solo.

CLAUDE DEBUSSY

3836

FASCINATION

F. D. MARCHETTI

TESORO MIO

E. BECUCCI

STAR OF THE EAST

2 bar piano intro
precedes solo.

AMANDA KENNEDY

Moderato

AURA LEE

Moderato

GEORGE POULTON

THEN YOU'LL REMEMBER ME

2 3/4 bar piano intro
precedes solo

Andante

M. W. BALFE

7096

MEDLEY OF CHRISTMAS CAROLS
WE THREE KINGS OF ORIENT ARE
JOHN H. HOPKINS

4 bar piano intro
precedes solo.

HARK, THE HERALD ANGELS SING
FELIX MENDELSSOHN

2 bar piano intro
precedes solo.

7096

AWAY IN A MANGER

JAMES R. MURRAY

2 beats piano intro
precedes solo.

SILENT NIGHT

FRANZ GRUBER

O COME ALL YE FAITHFUL

J. READING

1 3/4 bar piano intro
precedes solo.

7096

LA PALOMA

SEBASTIAN YRADIER

O SOLE MIO

EDUARDO DI CAPUA

7096

ROMANY LIFE

2 bar piano intro
precedes solo.

Allegro

VICTOR HERBERT

BLUE BELLS OF SCOTLAND

1 3/4 bar piano intro
precedes solo.

SCOTCH SONG

Moderato

ALL THROUGH THE NIGHT

2 bars piano music
precedes solo.

WELSH SONG

Moderato

7096

MERRY WIDOW WALTZ

8 bar piano intro
precedes solo.

FRANZ LEHAR

Waltz tempo

mf

3836

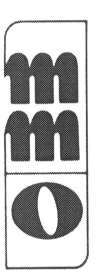

WORLD FAVORITES

MUSIC MINUS ONE • 50 Executive Boulevard • Elmsford, New York 10523-1325
Tel: (914) 592-1188   Fax: (914) 592-3116
E-mail: mmomus@aol.com   Websites: www.minusone.com *and* www.pocketsongs.com